D1563444

The art in this book was created from antique
Victorian greeting cards, postcards and other
decorative papers of the period. Artist Kathy Orr
combines these materials in collages in much the
same manner as Victorian ladies preserved favorite
mementos. It is hoped that this little volume will be
a cherished memento for you and your loved ones
for many Christmases to come.

Ed.

A Christmas Garland

Illustrated by Kathy Orr

Compiled by Julie Mitchell

The C.R. Gibson Company, Norwalk, Connecticut 06856

Peace and Love

Season's Cheer

Bells Across the Snow

O Christmas, merry Christmas!
Is it really come again,
With its memories and greetings,
With its joy and with its pain?
There's a minor in the carol,
And a shadow in the light,
And a spray of cypress twining
With the holly wreath to-night.
And the hush is never broken
By laughter light and low,
As we listen in the starlight
To the "bells across the snow."

O Christmas, merry Christmas!
'Tis not so very long
Since other voices blended
With the carol and the song!
If we could but hear them singing
As they are singing now,
If we could but see the radiance
Of the crown on each dear brow;
There would be no sigh to smother,
No hidden tear to flow,
As we listen in the starlight
To the "bells across the snow."

O Christmas, merry Christmas!
This never more can be;
We cannot bring again the days
Of our unshadowed glee.
But Christmas, happy Christmas,

Sweet herald of good-will,
With holy songs of glory
Brings holy gladness still.
For peace and hope may brighten,
And patient love may glow,
As we listen in the starlight
To the "bells across the snow."

Frances Ridley Havergal

Christmas at the Mill on the Floss

Fine old Christmas, with the snowy hair and ruddy face, had done his duty that year in the noblest fashion, and had set off his rich gifts of warmth and colour with all the heightening contrast of frost and snow.

Snow lay on the croft and river-bank in undulations softer than the limbs of infancy; it lay with the neatliest finished border on every sloping roof, making the dark-red gables stand out with a new depth of colour; it weighed heavily on the laurels and fir-trees till it fell from them with a shuddering sound; it clothed the rough turnip-field with whiteness, and made the sheep look like dark blotches; the gates were all blocked up with sloping drifts, and here and there a disregarded four-footed beast stood as if petrified "in unrecumbent sadness"; there was no gleam, no shadow, for the heavens, too, were one still, pale cloud—no sound or motion in anything but the dark river, that flowed and moaned like an unresting sorrow. But old Christmas smiled as he laid this cruel-seeming spell on the out-door world, for he meant to light up the home with new brightness, to deepen all the richness of indoor colour, and give a keener edge of delight to the warm fragrance of food: he meant to prepare a sweet imprisonment that would strengthen the primitive fellowship of kindred, and make the sunshine of familiar human faces as welcome as the hidden day-star. His kindness fell but hardly on the homeless—fell but hardly on the homes where the hearth was not very warm, and where the food had little fragrance; where the human faces had no sunshine in them, but rather the leaden, blank-eyed gaze of unexpectant want. But the fine old season meant well; and if he has not learnt the secret how to bless men impartially, it is because his father Time, with ever-unrelenting purpose, still hides that secret in his own mighty, slow-beating heart.

George Eliot

Heigh Ho, The Holly!

Blow, blow, thou winter wind—
Thou art not so unkind
As man's ingratitude!
Thy tooth is not so keen,
Because thou are not seen,
Although thy breath be rude.
Heigh ho! sing heigh ho! unto the green holly:
Most friendship is feigning, most loving mere folly.
Then heigh ho! the holly!
This life is most jolly!

Freeze, freeze, thou bitter sky—
Thou dost not bite so nigh
As benefits forgot!
Though thou the waters warp,
Thy sting is not so sharp
As friend remembered not.
Heigh ho! sing heigh ho! unto the green holly,
Most friendship is feigning, most loving mere folly.
Then heigh ho, the holly!
This life is most jolly!

William Shakespeare

A Christmas Carol

I care not for Spring; on his fickle wing
Let the blossoms and buds be borne:
He woos them amain with his treacherous rain,
And he scatters them ere the more.
An inconstant elf, he knows not himself,
Of his own changing mind an hour,
He'll smile in your face, and, with wry grimace,
He'll wither your youngest flower.

But song I'll troll out, for Christmas stout,
The hearty, the true, and the bold;
A bumper I drain, and with might and main
Give three cheers for this Christmas old.
We'll usher him in with a merry din
That shall gladden his joyous heart
And we'll keep him up while there's bite or sup,
And in fellowship good, we'll part.

Charles Dickens

Christmas Joy

A Christmas Carol

Scrooge and the Ghost of Christmas Present stood in the city streets on Christmas morning, where (for the weather was severe) the people made a rough but brisk and not unpleasant kind of music, in scraping snow from the pavement in front of their dwellings, and from the tops of their houses, whence it was mad delight to the boys to see it come plumping down into the road below, and splitting into artificial little snowstorms.

The people who were shovelling away on the housetops were jovial and full of glee, calling out to one another from the parapets, and now and then exchanging a facetious snowball—better-natured missile far than many a wordy jest—laughing heartily if it went right, and not less heartily if it went wrong.

But soon the steeples called good people all to church and chapel, and away they came, flocking through the streets in their best clothes, and with their gayest faces. And at the same time there emerged from scores of by-streets, lanes, and nameless turnings, innumerable people, carrying their dinners to the bakers' shops. The sight of these poor revellers appeared to interest the Spirit very much, for he stood, with Scrooge beside him, in a baker's doorway, and, taking off the covers as their bearers passed, sprinkled incense on their dinners from his torch. And it was a very uncommon kind of torch, for once or twice when there were angry words between some dinner-carriers who had jostled each other, he shed a few drops of water on them from it, and their good-humor was restored directly. For they said it was a shame to quarrel upon Christmas Day. And so it was! God love it, so it was!

In time the bells ceased, and the bakers were shut up; and yet there was a genial shadowing forth of all these dinners, and the progress of their cooking, in the thawed blotch of wet above each baker's oven, where the pavement smoked as if its stones were cooking too.

"Is there a peculiar flavour in what you sprinkle from your torch?" asked Scrooge.

"There is. My own."

"Would it apply to any kind of dinner on this day?" asked Scrooge.

"To any kindly given. To a poor one most."

"Why to a poor one most?" asked Scrooge.

"Because it needs it most."

They went on, invisible, as they had been before, into the suburbs of the town. It was a remarkable quality of the Ghost that, notwithstanding his gigantic size, he could accommodate himself to any place with ease; and that he stood beneath a low roof quite as gracefully, and like a supernatural creature, as it was possible he could have done in any lofty hall.

And perhaps it was the pleasure the good Spirit had in showing off this power of his, or else it was his own kind, generous, hearty nature, and his sympathy with all poor men, that led him straight to Scrooge's clerk's; for there he went, and took Scrooge with him, holding to his robe; and on the threshold of the door the Spirit smiled, and stopped to bless Bob Cratchit's dwelling with sprinklings of his torch. Think of that! Bob had but fifteen "bob" a week himself; he pocketed on Saturdays but fifteen copies of his Christian name; and yet the Ghost of Christmas Present blessed his four-roomed house!

Such a bustle ensued that you might have thought a goose the rarest of all birds—a feathered phenomenon, to which a black swan was a matter of course—and in truth it was something very like it in that house. Mrs. Cratchit made the gravy hissing hot; Master Peter mashed the potatoes with incredible vigour; Miss Belinda sweetened up the apple-sauce; Martha dusted the hot plates; Bob took Tiny Tim beside him in a tiny corner at the table; the two young Cratchits set chairs for everybody, not forgetting themselves, and mounting guard upon their posts, crammed spoons into their mouths, lest they should shriek for goose before their turn came to be helped. At last the dishes were set on, and grace was said. It was succeeded by a breathless pause, as Mrs. Cratchit, looking slowly all along the carving knife, prepared to plunge it into the breast; but when she did, and when the long expected gush of stuffing issued forth, one murmur of delight arose all round the board, and even Tiny Tim, excited by the two young Cratchits, beat on the table with the handle of his knife, and feebly cried, "Hurrah!"

There was never such a goose. Bob said he didn't believe there ever was such a goose cooked. Its tenderness and flavour, size and cheapness, were the themes of universal admiration. Eked out by apple-sauce and mashed potatoes, it was a sufficient dinner for the whole family; indeed, as Mrs. Cratchit said with great delight (surveying one small atom of a bone upon the dish), they hadn't ate it all at last! Yet every one had had enough, and the youngest Cratchits in particular were steeped in sage and onion to the eyebrows! But now, the plates being changed by Miss Belinda, Mrs. Cratchit left the room alone—too nervous to bear witness—to take the pudding up and bring it in.

Oh, a wonderful pudding! Bob Cratchit said, and calmly, too, that he regarded it as the greatest success achieved by

Mrs. Cratchit since their marriage. Mrs. Cratchit said that, now the weight was off her mind, she would confess she had her doubts about the quantity of flour. Everybody had something to say about it, but nobody thought or said it was at all a small pudding for a large family. It would have been flat heresy to do so. Any Cratchit would have blushed to hint at such a thing.

At last dinner was all done, the cloth was cleared, the hearth swept, and the fire made up. The compound in the jug being tasted, and considered perfect, apples and oranges were put on the table, and a shovelful of chestnuts on the fire. Then all the Cratchit family drew round the hearth in what Bob Cratchit called a circle, meaning half a one; and at Bob Cratchit's elbow stood the family display of glass—two tumblers and a custard cup without a handle.

These held the hot stuff from the jug, however, as well as golden goblets would have done; and Bob served it out with beaming looks, while the chestnuts on the fire sputtered and cracked noisily. Then Bob proposed: "A Merry Christmas to us all, my dears. God bless us!" Which all the family reechoed.

"God bless us every one!" said Tiny Tim, the last of all.

Charles Dickens

Merry Christmas

In the rush of early morning,
When the red burns through the gray,
And the wintry world lies waiting
For the glory of the day.
Then we hear a fitful rustling
Just without upon the stair,
See two small white phantoms coming,
Catch the gleam of sunny hair.

Are they Christmas fairies stealing
Rows of little socks to fill?
Are they angels floating hither
With their message of good-will?
What sweet spell are these elves weaving,
As like larks they chirp and sing?
Are these palms of peace from heaven
That these lovely spirits bring?

Rosy feet upon the threshold,
Eager faces peeping through,
With the first red ray of sunshine,
Chanting cherubs come in view;
Mistletoe and gleaming holly,
Symbols of a blessed day,
In their chubby hands they carry,
Streaming all along the way.

Well we know them, never weary
Of this innocent surprise;
Waiting, watching, listening always
With full hearts and tender eyes,
While our little household angels,
White and golden in the sun,
Greet us with the sweet old welcome—
"Merry Christmas, every one!"

Louisa May Alcott

O Christmas Tree

To a Christmas Tree

*O balsam tree, that lately held
The stars like nesting birds among
Your emerald branches, listen now
To children's voices sweet with song!*

*You talker with the wind, and friend
Of fox and fawn and silver mouse,
Bearing your tinsel and your gifts,
Glow softly now within this house,*

*Bringing your fragrance to our hearts,
Assuring us that wars will cease.
For a Child's bright birthday shine with faith,
O tree of loveliness and peace!*

Frances Frost

The Miracle of the Fir Tree

Once upon a time on a frosty Christmas Eve, in a small village, a little boy was wandering barefooted, from house to house.

"Would anyone like to buy two small fir trees?... You can decorate them with bright lights and paper stars... It's a lot of fun for the children," the boy would cry, as he knocked on a door.

At each house, the answer was always the same:

"You've come too late, child. We've already bought our Christmas tree. Come back again next year."

And each time the boy would go away with tears in his eyes. If he didn't sell the two trees there would be nothing for his family to eat. His mother and father were both sick, and his two brothers were still babies. Albert was the only one in his family able to earn money. So, in spite of the bitter cold, he roved through the street, looking for someone to buy his fir trees. He had found the trees on the edge of the woods, just as night began to fall, at the hour when hungry wolves began their howling.

After knocking on several doors, and receiving many blunt answers, the boy found himself at the house of Eidel, the gardener.

Can you imagine trying to sell fir trees to a man whose job is to make them grow?

Albert knocked.

"Who is knocking at this hour?" Eidel's gruff voice replied.

By now, Albert was so afraid, he didn't dare say who he was or what he wanted.

"Who is it? Who is knocking at my door when I want to be left in peace?" grumbled Eidel, his wooden shoes clattering as he came along.

When the door opened the boy saw a beautiful tree, glistening with gaily wrapped presents and decorations whose bright glittering lit up the deserted street. At the other end of the room, there was a blazing fire in the hearth. And sitting near it were three children looking from the hearth to the kitchen where a juicy Christmas turkey lay on a table just waiting to be eaten.

"What do you want little one?" Eidel asked the boy. "What are you doing with those two stunted fir trees?"

Albert didn't answer, as he thought he had just lost his chance to earn money.

"The cold wind is blowing in," said the gardener. "Speak up, boy, or I'll have to close the door and leave you standing there."

Looking at the poor, frightened Albert standing in the snow, without any shoes, the gardener thought of his own children. They were about the same age as this boy. "If I were not here to look after them, some wintry night, my children might be roaming the streets too," he said to himself. But kindly he asked Albert, "What can I do for you?"

"I wanted to sell my fir trees for Christmas," said Albert, "but you already have such a beautiful one."

"Never mind!" Eidel answered. "All the same, I'll buy yours." And he went to get a gold coin from the drawer where he kept his savings.

"It's too good to be true," thought Albert. "The old gardener must be playing a joke on me, or maybe it's all a dream." But when each of the children gave him a slice of turkey and their mother brought out a piping hot bowl of soup, Albert knew he wasn't dreaming.

When he had finished eating, the boy thanked the kind gardener and his family. And, happy as a lark, he started home with Eidel's dog for protection against the wolves.

On Christmas morning, after all the presents had been opened, Mrs. Eidel started cleaning up her house. She picked up all the wrappings, the ribbons, the decorations, and put them away. Then she threw the two fir trees of Albert's into the street.

Her three children were playing in the street while waiting to go to church. When they saw their mother throw the fir trees out they decided to pretend they were gardeners, just like their father. So they took the trees across the road and planted them behind the church.

Soon the church bells began to ring and crowds of people started pouring into the church. Eidel and his family were among the first to arrive. Dressed in his best clothes, Eidel sat with his wife and children in the front pew. The gardener reverently asked God to watch over his family. As the choir sang the glory and wonder of Our Lord's birth, it occurred to Eidel that the infant born in a manger is the true brother of poor children. "One can never be too kind to them," the gardener thought.

Mass was over, the candles snuffed out and the last parishioners leaving, when, all at once, the crowd outside the church gasped in amazement. High above the steeple, as straight as masts of a ship, were two fir trees, towering to the sky. And all around their thick, heavy branches, doves, as white as snow, singing the Glory of God.

Jean Variot
Translated from the French
by Leon King

The Mahogany-Tree

Christmas is here;
Winds whistle shrill,
Icy and chill,
Little care we;
Little we fear
Weather without,
Sheltered about
The Mahogany-Tree.

Once on the boughs
Birds of rare plume
Sang in its bloom;
Night-birds are we;
Here we carouse,
Singing, like them,
Perched round the stem
Of the jolly old tree.

Here let us sport,
Boys, as we sit—
Laughter and wit
Flashing so free.
Life is but short—
When we are gone,
Let them sing on,
Round the old tree.

Evenings we knew,
Happy as this;
Faces we miss,
Pleasant to see.
Kind hearts and true,
Gentle and just,
Peace to your dust!
We sing round the tree.

Care like a dun,
Lurks at the gate;
Let the dog wait;
Happy we'll be!
Drink, every one;
Pile up the coals;
Fill the red bowls,
Round the old tree!

Drain we the cup—
Friend, art afraid?
Spirits are laid
In the Red Sea.
Mantle it up;
Empty it yet;
Let us forget,
Round the old tree!

Sorrows begone!
Life and its ills,
Duns and their bills,
Bid we to flee.
Come with the dawn,
Blue-devil sprite;
Leave us tonight,
Round the old tree!

William Makepeace Thackeray

To The Fir-Tree

O Fir-tree green! O Fir-tree green!
Your leaves are constant ever,
Not only in the summer time,
But through the winter's snow and rime
O Fir-tree green! O Fir-tree green!
You're green and fresh forever.

O Fir-tree green! O Fir-tree green!
I still shall love you dearly!
How oft to me on Christmas night
Your laden boughs have brought delight.
O Fir-tree green! O Fir-tree green!
I shall love you dearly.

From the German

Dear Santa Claus

A Visit From St. Nicholas

'Twas the night before Christmas,
when all through the house
Not a creature was stirring, not even a mouse;
The stockings were hung by the chimney with care,
In hopes that St. Nicholas soon would be there;
The children were nestled all sung in their beds,
While visions of sugar-plums danced in their heads;
And Mamma in her 'kerchief, and I in my cap,
Had just settled our brains for a long winter's nap, —
When out of the lawn there arose such a clatter,
I sprang from my bed to see what was the matter;
Away to the window I flew like a flash,
Tore open the shutters and threw up the sash.
The moon on the breast of the new-fallen snow
Gave the luster of midday to objects below;
When, what to my wondering eyes should appear,
But a miniature sleigh, and eight tiny reindeer,
With a little old driver, so lively and quick,
I knew in a moment it must be Saint Nick.
More rapid than eagles his coursers they came,
And he whistled, and shouted, and called them by name:
"Now, Dasher! now, Dancer! now, Prancer and Vixen!
On, Comet! on, Cupid! on, Donder and Blitzen!
To the top of the porch! to the top of the wall!
Now, dash away! dash away! dash away all!"
As dry leaves that before the wild hurricane fly,
When they meet with an obstacle, mount to the sky,
So up to the house-top the coursers they flew,
With a sleigh full of toys — and St. Nicholas too!
And then, in a twinkling, I heard on the roof,

The prancing and pawing of each little hoof.
As I drew in my head, and was turning around,
Down the chimney St. Nicholas came with a bound.
He was dressed all in fur, from his head to his foot,
And his clothes were all tarnished with ashes and soot!
A bundle of toys he had flung on his back,
And he looked like a peddler just opening his pack;
His eyes—how they twinkled! his dimples, how merry!
His cheeks were like roses, his nose like a cherry!
His droll little mouth was drawn up like a bow,
And the beard of his chin was as white as the snow.
The stump of his pipe he held tight in his teeth,
And the smoke, it encircled his head like a wreath.
He had a broad face, and a little round belly,
That shook, when he laugh'd like a bowl full of jelly.
He was chubby and plump; a right jolly old elf;
And I laughed, when I saw him, in spite of myself.
A wink of his eye, and a twist of his head,
Soon gave me to know I had nothing to dread.
He spoke not a word, but went straight to his work,
And filled all the stockings—then turned with a jerk,
And laying his finger aside his nose,
And giving a nod, up the chimney he rose.
He sprang to his sleigh, to his team gave a whistle,
And away they all flew, like the down of a thistle.
But I heard him exclaim, ere he drove out of sight,
"Happy Christmas to all! and to all a good night!"

Clement C. Moore

Santa Claus

He comes in the night! He comes in the night!
He softly, silently comes,
While the sweet little heads on the pillows so white
Are dreaming of bugles and drums.
He cuts through the snow like a ship through the foam,
While the white flakes 'round him whirl.
Who tells him I know not, but he finds the home
Of each good little boy and girl.

Anonymous, 1880

Kriss Kringle

Just as the moon was fading amid her misty rings,
And every stocking was stuffed with childhood's precious things,
Old Kriss Kringle looked round, and on an elm-tree bough,
High-hung, an oriole's nest, silent and empty now.
"Quite like a stocking," he laughed, "pinned up there on the tree!
Little I thought the birds expected a present from me!"
Then old Kriss Kringle who loves a joke as well as the best,
Dropped a handful of flakes in the oriole's empty nest.

Thomas Bailey Aldrich

An editorial reprint from the New York Sun:

September 21, 1897

We take pleasure in answering at once and thus prominently the communication below, expressing at the same time our great gratification that its faithful author is numbered among the friends of The Sun:

Dear Editor:
I am 8 years old. Some of my little friends say there is no Santa Claus. Papa says "If you see it in The Sun it's so." Please tell me the truth, is there a Santa Claus?

Virginia O'Hanlon
115 West 95th Street
New York City

Yes, Virginia, there is a Santa Claus. He exists as certainly as love, and generosity and devotion exist, and you know that they abound and give to your life its highest beauty and joy. Alas! how dreary would be the world if there were no Santa Claus! It would be as dreary as if there were no Virginias...

No Santa Claus! Thank God he lives, and he lives forever. A thousand years from now, Virginia, nay, ten times ten thousand years from now, he will continue to make glad the heart of childhood.

Francis P. Church

Christmas Wonder

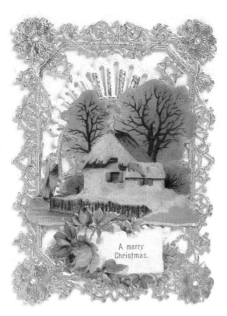

A merry
Christmas.

A Christmas Carol

Everywhere, everywhere, Christmas tonight!
Christmas in lands of the fir-tree and pine,
Christmas in lands of the palm-tree and vine,
Christmas where snow-peaks stand solemn and white,
Christmas where corn-fields lie sunny and bright;
Everywhere, everywhere, Christmas tonight!

Christmas where children are hopeful and gay,
Christmas where old men are patient and gray;
Christmas where peace, like a dove in its flight,
Broods o'er men in the thick of the fight;
Everywhere, everywhere, Christmas tonight!

So the stars of the midnight which compass us round
Shall see a strange glory, and hear a sweet sound,
And, cry "Look! the earth is aflame with delight,
O sons of the morning rejoice at the sight."
Everywhere, everywhere, Christmas tonight!

Phillips Brooks

The Touch of Angel's Wings

It was Christmas Eve. Elizabeth sat on the edge of her little daughter's bed. She bent over and kissed the rose-petaled cheek. With golden-flax hair spreading over the pillow and long lashes heavy with sleep, Marya looked for all the world like an angel.

Elizabeth's heart swelled with love and overflowed with the sweet joy of sharing. On this, the holiest night, she had told her little daughter about the visit of the angel.

The two of them had sat listening to the delicate Swedish chimes and watching the little angels dance round and round above the glow of magical candles. The first Christmas after Marya was born, Elizabeth's mother had given her the family keepsake. "Because you always loved it so," her mother had said.

Earlier, as Elizabeth saw the glow of candles reflected in her little daughter's blue eyes, she felt the tender excitement mounting until the two of them and the candles were one. And Elizabeth knew it was time to share her marvelous secret.

With joy swelling even greater Elizabeth remembered the first Christmas the angel had given her the joy of the Christmas season.

She was about Marya's age the evening she sat at the table long after the dishes had been cleared away. With her chin cupped in her hands, she followed the movement of the angels and the light tinkling of the chimes.

"Elizabeth is enchanted by those angel chimes," her mother announced to no one in particular.

It was that night Elizabeth was awakened by the soft whir-r-r.

Moonlight shimmered through the curtains of her bedroom window like the lace on her grandmother's dresses. Elizabeth lay very still. Then in the soft darkness she saw the angel—one of them from the chimes—moving around her room. Moonlight frosted the tips of the angel's wings and the tiny horn by her mouth made the softest of sound like twinkling bits of laughter.

Suddenly a silver magic enveloped the room, making Elizabeth's heart tremble. But she was not afraid. Under covers streaked by moonlight she marveled at the angel's fluttering. She saw the gossamer wings brush the dolls on the trunk against the wall, her dollhouse, the edges of her storybooks, her clothes. And with the touch the whole room became a place of heavenly sweetness.

And then quietly as the enchantment had come, it disappeared. The whirring stopped and the angel was gone. Yet a glory shone over the room until Elizabeth fell asleep again.

The next morning, it was as if the angel's wings had cleansed and blessed the world. How new everything looked! The faces of her dolls were clear and bright. Even the air smelled clean. It was as if Elizabeth was seeing and feeling everything for the first time. Her whole world was different—it had been touched by the angel's wings.

Eager to share, she had burst into the kitchen where her parents and brothers had already gathered around the breakfast table.

"Last night," she began, pointing to the little angels standing frozen in their angelic poses, "one of the angels came to my room and—"

"Yeah, Elizabeth—" Her brothers' laughter cut across her beautiful story.

"Boys!" her mother reprimanded. "Elizabeth has a vivid imagination." And Elizabeth thought she detected a trace of a smile at the corner of her father's mouth.

Even so, the angel's touch filled the Christmas season with wonder and magic. On other Christmases the angel's coming was never quite the same. Once or twice she heard the whirring or the faint tooting of the horn. Another time she saw the moonlight frosting gossamer wings in flight. But Elizabeth knew the little angel always came and that the coming gave the world a special glow of miracles.

And tonight, after carrying this beautiful secret in her heart for all these years, she had shared it with her very own little girl. Now the beauty and magic of the angel's touch would live forever as it passed from heart to heart in love.

Those without faith might say it was just a dream, but Elizabeth knew that she had been chosen by God to be blessed with the gift of the angel's visit. For only those who believe can know the touch of the angel's wings and the miracles it brings. For in them Christ is born again each Christmas.

Perhaps tonight Marya would be awakened by the soft whir of wings.

Idella Bodie

Christmas Greeting
from a Fairy to a Child

Lady, dear, if Fairies may
For a moment lay aside
Cunning tricks and elfish play,
'Tis at happy Christmas-tide.

We have heard the children say —
Gentle children, whom we love —
Long ago on Christmas Day,
Came a message from above.

Still, as Christmas-tide comes round,
They remember it again —
Echo still the joyful sound
"Peace on earth, good-will to men!"

Lewis Carroll

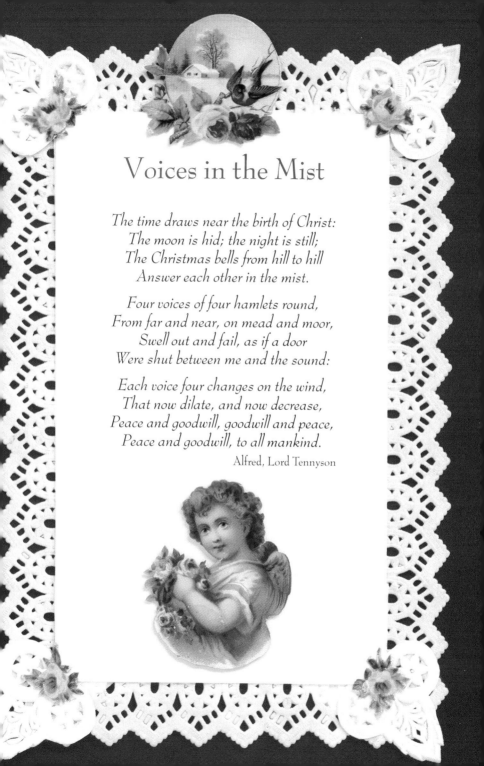

Voices in the Mist

The time draws near the birth of Christ:
The moon is hid; the night is still;
The Christmas bells from hill to hill
Answer each other in the mist.

Four voices of four hamlets round,
From far and near, on mead and moor,
Swell out and fail, as if a door
Were shut between me and the sound:

Each voice four changes on the wind,
That now dilate, and now decrease,
Peace and goodwill, goodwill and peace,
Peace and goodwill, to all mankind.

Alfred, Lord Tennyson

Heaven Cannot Hold Him

*In the bleak mid-winter
Frosty wind made moan,
Earth stood hard as iron,
Water like a stone;
Snow had fallen, snow on snow,
Snow on snow,
In the bleak mid-winter
Long ago.*

*Our God, Heaven cannot hold Him
Nor earth sustain;
Heaven and earth shall flee away,
When He comes to reign.
In the bleak mid-winter
A stable-place sufficed
The Lord God Almighty,
Jesus Christ.*

*Angels and archangels
May have gathered there;
Cherubim and seraphim
Thronged the air.
But only His Mother,
In her maiden bliss,
Worshipped her Beloved
With a kiss.*

*What can I give Him,
Poor as I am?
If I were a shepherd
I would bring a lamb;
If I were a wise man,
I would do my part, —
Yet what I can I give Him,
Give my heart.*

Christina G. Rossetti

Child Jesus

When the Christ-Child to this world came down,
He left for us His throne and crown,
He lay in a manger, all pure and fair,
Of straw and hay His bed so bare.
But high in heaven the star shone bright,
And the oxen watched by the Babe that night.
Hallelujah! Child Jesus!

Oh, come, ye sinful and ye who mourn,
Forgetting all your sin and sadness,
In the city of David a Child is born,
Who doth bring us heav'nly gladness.
Then let us to the manger go,
To see the Christ who hath loved us so.
Hallelujah! Christ Jesus!

Hans Christian Andersen

The Three Kings

Three Kings came riding from far away,
Melchior and Gaspar and Baltasar;
Three Wise Men out of the East were they,
And they traveled by night and they slept by day,
For their guide was a beautiful, wonderful star.

The star was so beautiful, large and clear,
That all the other stars of the sky
Became a white mist in the atmosphere;
And by this they knew that the coming was near
Of the Prince foretold in the prophecy.

Three caskets they bore on their saddle-bows,
Three caskets of gold with golden keys;
Their robes were of crimson silk, with rows
Of bells and pomegranates and furbelows,
Their turbans like blossoming almond-trees.

And so the Three Kings rode into the West,
Through the dusk of night over hill and dell,
And sometimes they nodded with beard on breast,
And sometimes talked, as they paused to rest,
With people they met at some wayside well.

"Of the Child that is born," said Baltasar,
"Good people, I pray you, tell us the news;
For we in the East have seen His star,
And have ridden fast, and have ridden far,
To find and worship the King of the Jews."

And the people answered, "You ask in vain;
We know of no king but Herod the Great!"
They thought the Wise Men were men insane,

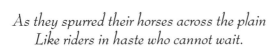

As they spurred their horses across the plain
Like riders in haste who cannot wait.

And when they came to Jerusalem,
Herod the Great, who had heard this thing,
Sent for the Wise Men and questioned them;
And said, "Go down unto Bethlehem,
And bring me tidings of this new king."

So they rode away, and the star stood still,
The only one in the gray of the morn;
Yes, it stopped, it stood still of its own free will,
Right over Bethlehem on the hill,
The city of David where Christ was born.

And the Three Kings rode through the gate and the guard,
Through the silent street, till their horses turned
And neighed as they entered the great inn-yard;
But the windows were closed, and the doors were barred,
And only a light in the stable burned.

And cradled there in the scented hay,
In the air made sweet by the breath of kine,
The little Child in the manger lay,
The Child that would be King one day
Of a kingdom not human, but divine.

Henry Wadsworth Longfellow

Ring Out the Old

Ring out the old, ring in the new,
Ring, happy bells, across the snow;
The year is going, let him go;
Ring out the false, ring in the true.

Ring out the grief that saps the mind,
For those that here we see no more;
Ring out the feud of rich and poor,
Ring in redress to all mankind.

Ring out a slowly dying cause,
And ancient forms of party strife;
Ring in the nobler modes of life,
With sweeter manners, purer laws.

Ring out the want, the care, the sin,
The faithless coldness of times;
Ring out, ring out my mournful rhymes,
But ring the fuller minstrel in.

Ring out false pride in place and blood,
The civic slander and the spite;
Ring in the love of truth and right,
Ring in the common love of good.

Ring out old shapes of foul disease;
Ring out the narrowing lust of gold;
Ring out the thousand wars of old,
Ring in a thousand years of peace.

Ring in the valiant man and free,
The larger heart, the kindlier hand;
Ring out the darkness of the land,
Ring in the Christ that is to be.

Alfred Tennyson

Colophon
Designed by Robert Pantelone
Typeset in Bernhard Modern and
Bernhard Modern Italic